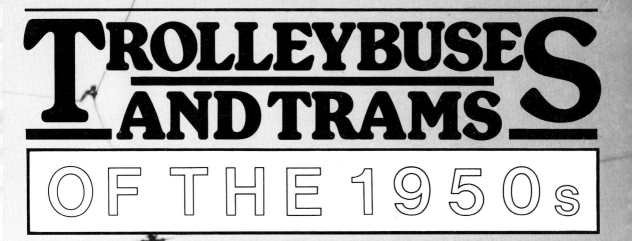

TROLLEYBUSES AND TRAMS

OF THE 1950s

JULIAN THOMPSON

LONDON

IAN ALLAN LTD

First published 1982

ISBN 0 7110 1181 8

Design by Robert C. Wilcockson

© Ian Allan Ltd 1982

Published by Ian Allan Ltd, Shepperton, Surrey;
and printed by Ian Allan Printing Ltd at their works
at Coombelands in Runnymede, England

Cover: London Transport trolleybuses at
Stratford Broadway in July 1959.

Cover, inset: Sheffield car No 222 at
Tinsley in March 1960.

CONTENTS

FOREWORD

When school was out in 1945 my idea of heaven was to ride a car from Balham to Stockwell and back. My four-page *Evening News* I read in the topdeck rear seat, as the rails unwound faster than if I sat up front.

I didn't know what made the system tick, but it fascinated me from the word go. Soon I built balsawood replicas that fitted in a matchbox. It was a close call the day my bicycle wheel went down the slot, but the United bus had good brakes! I realised the conduit or slot system was worth a hard look. But it was a while before I rode a line where the cars clung to the wire like a cablecar hooks on the cable.

In 1946 I used Kingsway Tunnel to Pitman's College. The 1938 map there was my only system guide. By 1947 I'd ridden the whole network. One of my last finds was 58 from Camberwell to Greenwich. The first trip the conductor asked when I was getting out. I didn't know either. The car climbed and curved, it had no sooner topped one hill than there was another steep grade. The scenic and speedy 58 with its HR/2s became my pet route. It's a shame the 100 HR/2s were scrapped except for three sold to Leeds. I never dreamed that one day people would pay high fares for short trips on such cars at museums.

In early post-World War 2 London, the car swayed along streets past food lines in threadbare apparel. How dismal, you will say. But not for us. Shortages meant scrapping was delayed. Now austerity is a dirty word, but for buffs it meant variety in transport. London had 10 different car types from seven operators. Even then there were people who nostalgised over the lost past. So they missed the unique present of 30 years ago!

On my first system visit outside London at Easter 1947, the car rumbled from Piccadilly to Hazel Grove, passing Stockport lines on route. Manchester was the first big city to run down its trams, and it meant just that. Manchester's 1949 closure had a pyschologic effect on the press, but London didn't close next day! That summer in Southampton I stared in stunned disbelief at opentoppers with wood seats and open fronts. Next year the cars were in St Denys scrapyard. Efforts to museumise an oldtimer would have been better spent saving the system. Southampton cars had survived Hitler's bombing, but protests against scrapping were ineffective.

The Leeds guest house I stayed at in 1948 was a car ride from City Hall. Transportwise Leeds was unprogressive apart from some fine right-of-way. The varied fleet had many used cars from other cities. Sheffield had everything going for it. The car development policy culminated in the Roberts type. I was lucky to ride on the Sheffield to Rotherham interurban before the line closed in 1949. That was the worst post-World War 2 year for British systems. After reading in the Leeds paper that Bradford cars were hit by a thunderstorm, I hotfooted it next day to see the light blue, open balcony cars. Riding down the steep grades was a hair-raising experience.

The clacking of cars through Grafton Street switch tongues woke me each morning on my first Edinburgh visit in 1949. The staid paint-scheme of the cars with their lightcode at night matched the monumental city. Edinburgh vied with Sheffield in efficiency but lacked right-of-way. Track maintenance slumped from the early 1950s. On a Glasgow side trip I still recall the new-smell of just-built Cunarders. These most luxurious of all British cars could still be running. Operation was slick and track well kept.

In London, depots were being razed and rebuilt. Even as first closures neared, cars were still being overhauled and track relaid. Hectic activity at County Hall meant a whole new layout, swansong of the conduit system. This last fling of the conduit system has been little documented. Maybe Herbert Morrison was right to fume that it was money wasted, but I'm glad nobody listened. In 1950 County Hall was a magnet for me even in my lunchbreak. The layout proved conduit track could give a smooth ride. It's a shame that track good for 10 years was used for only two.

Yes, the conduit system got the big end of the stick. In 1947-52 I rode over 18,000 miles on such track and don't recall my car ever broke its plough. There were many weather-induced plough breaks, and sometimes wheels went one way at junctions and ploughs another. T-rails were regularly checked by men toting longhandled mirrors. But London Transport couldn't be expected to fund rebuilding of condemned plant.

At the first London route closures of 1 October 1950, return and transfer fares were axed. Tickets were miniscule works of art and simplified issue another step toward mediocrity. At this time there was much activity to have scrapping shelved. A vain hope, you may say, to protest at LT's policy, but a handful of idealists wouldn't have wanted it any other way. A lot of leather was worn out delivering handbills. Public response was stillborn as LT refused to waive its policy and refused to try out a modern car. Undaunted fans fought to save the shrinking system until the last wheel turned on a summer night in 1952. Next day, we couldn't grasp that the still shiny rails would never be used again!

One of the most active workers for retention was John Walton of Clapham. He had used the cars for 20 years and gave me insight into operations. I still recall how he'd race over Clapham High Street at 8.30am, daring any motor driver to hinder boarding passengers, to join me on the Embankment-bound car. John shamed others who had no time or energy to protest against scrapping plans. Despite foot problems, he was always on call. He never tired of saying that LCC cars never made a working loss. It's easy to claim nothing could have saved the system. Much blame must attach to a gullible public that went along with LT's views. The story that LT couldn't afford to fund operations after 1933 is now hallowed transport mythology.

The Birmingham narrow gauge network closed 1953. It was well maintained but had no new plant. Londoners could no longer ride the cars on a day trip, given the then train schedules. By 1955 even Edinburgh, Leeds, Liverpool, and Sheffield had shrunk. Most of Glasgow was intact, but closure of outboundary lines in 1957 meant curtains for a fine system.

Sheffield rolling stock had been consistently updated and new cars built. Good track and right-of-way links made it on all counts the best British system. Even Sheffield was only treading water, and before the last Roberts car was delivered, it decided to scrap. The well organised campaign for retention failed, and now Sheffield regrets the loss of light rail transit. Trolleybuses proved a non-starter in Glasgow, where trams were phased out over 14 years, but most lines closed 1956-62. The progressive policy down to 1950 collapsed, with the bizarre result that lines closed to release old cars for the scrapyard!

Government policy of frowning on electric street transport meant the flimsiest of excuses were offered for scrapping. Sheffield had traffic problems. Co-ordination of services in Edinburgh was possible only if trams went. By the early 1950s traffic growth made life difficult and hindered city transport. But the government sat on its hands while the country slid toward total oil reliance.

Trolleybus closure didn't stir much dust. It wasn't until 1954 that a system decorated the last bus — Southend. Down to 1954 only five post-World War 2 installations had gone. In the 1950s 10 went, and in the 1960s 22, leaving only four. These had a free hand to scrap, as equipment and extra parts were unavailable.

For small towns loss of trolleybuses meant the end of quiet, fumeless, and efficient transit. Often pride in local transport went with trams and trolleybuses too. Motor buses signalled an era of skyrocketing inflation with higher fares.

Government-approved waste of resources means most British road transport is oil-fuelled. There is slim chance electric road vehicles will return. Trams are too costly for cities to start restoring lost facilities. There is also the problem of finding makers.

Must local transport always worsen? Yes, until the vehicle is fitted for its task as it once was. There can be no return to custom-built designs of the past and only standardisation can help bring back trams and trolleybuses. New cars for trunk city lines would be articulateds, with trolleybuses for light traffic. Flat fares and passes are essential for ease of operation and usership. Resistance to modern, proven methods must still be overcome.

Acknowledgements

To Mr E. R. Stone FLA, Librarian of the Transport Trust Library at University of Guildford.

To Dr Gerald Druce, for allowing reproduction of his photographs and supplying valuable information.

BIBLIOGRAPHY

ABC Birmingham Transport, W. A. Camwell
Buses
Buses Illustrated
Edinburgh's Transport, D. L. G. Hunter
Great British Tramway Networks, W. H. Bett and
  J. C. Gillham
History of the British Trolleybus, J. Owen
London Transport Tramways Handbook,
  D. W. Willoughby and E. R. Oakley

London Trolleybus, Dryhurst Publications
London's Trolleybuses, Omnibus Society
Maidstone Trolleybus, D. J. S. Scotney
Modern Tramway
Public Transport in Ipswich, R. Markham
Railway Magazine
Trolleybus Magazine

ABERDEEN

Left: The last half-mile of the Hazlehead line was a right-of-way. Ex-Manchester Pilcher car No 52 of 1930 design passes Woodend bound for Sea Beach. In 1956 the Hazlehead line closed and the last Pilchers were withdrawn. (16.6.54)

Below: Luxury streamliner No 27, one of 20 built in 1949 with Pickering body and EMB trucks, lays over at Bridge of Don terminus on route 1. This last route closed in 1958. (16.6.54)

BELFAST

Left: A Belfast McCreary car shows its clean lines at Ardoyne depot north-west of the city. Fifty McCrearys were built from 1935. Edinburgh, Liverpool, Sheffield, and Belfast were the only cities with large fleets of single-truck cars. The Belfast system closed in 1954. (17.6.53)

BIRMINGHAM

Right: Car No 774 has just arrived at Rednal from Navigation Street. Built as a totally enclosed car with air-wheel brakes by Brush in 1926, No 774 changed little during its working life. This type of car seated 60 or 62. A confusing feature of the system for strangers was the method of identifying destinations by route number. No destination was shown at the ends, and side displays gave outer terminals only. Sometimes a number was used in one direction only from several terminals. Cars from Pype Hayes, Erdington, or Short Heath to Gravelly Hill all showed 59. (20.4.52)

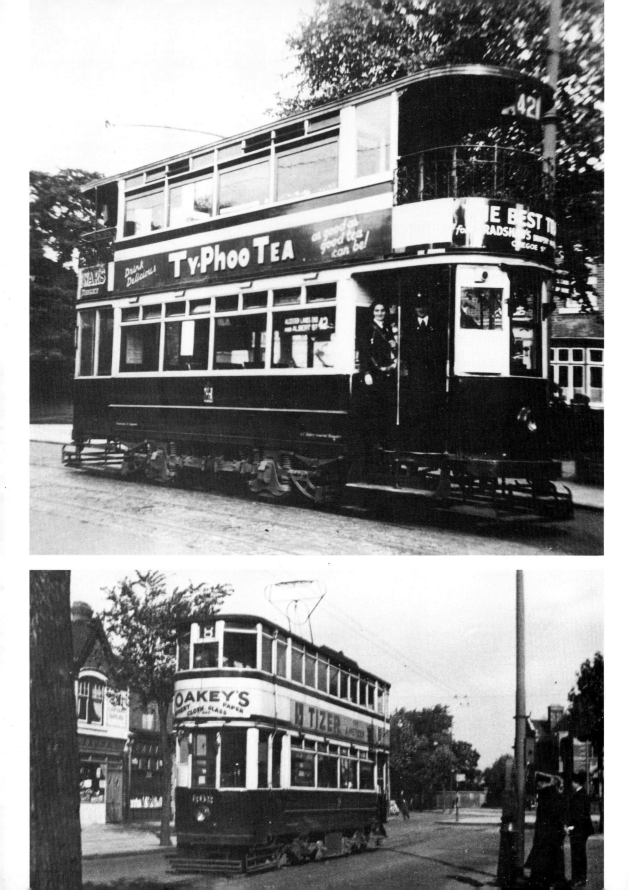

Left: The crew of spotless Birmingham No 405 built in 1912 pose at Alcester Lanes End. Most of these cars lasted until Moseley Road lines closed one week after the photo was taken. (25.9.49)

Below left: Regulators watch as stately Birmingham No 802 reverses at Alum Rock on a Sunday two weeks before buses take over. The Alum Rock and Washwood Heath lines were worked by bowcollector cars. Birmingham's cars were always well kept and smooth running. (17.9.50)

Right: Birmingham's only modern cars were Nos 841 and 842. No 842 was a lightweight metal car built in 1929 by Short Bros on English Electric airbraked trucks. Smart navy-blue and yellow No 842 is seen at Cotteridge Depot yard. (20.4.52)

Below: From left to right cars Nos 734, 736, and 773 stand before Selly Oak depot. Cars from here serviced the Bristol Road routes. They linked industry, residential districts and pleasant countryside. Rednal and Rubery terminals were well laid out and had turning circles and waiting facilities. No 773 was a onetime bowcollector car on the Alum Rock and Washwood Heath lines. (20.4.52)

BLACKPOOL

Left: Coronation No 314 lays over at Fleetwood Ferry, at the north end of the line. These cars were introduced in 1952 and 25 were built. They were 50ft long and with 180hp motors, were among Britain's most powerful. Design problems blunted their success. Most were withdrawn after 15 years. Behind No 314 is a 1933-type Railcoach. (15.6.56)

Below left: Blackpool's 1933 railcoaches, like these two at Bispham, were an innovative British design. Over 75 were built up to 1939. Head car No 303 has resilient wheel trucks with inside bearing axles. (15.6.56)

Above: Coronation No 314 of 1952 design heads south to South Promenade in the late evening on Queens Drive at Uncle Tom's Cabin. (15.6.56)

Below: 1933-Type Railcoach Nos 293 and 276 in variations of green and cream are about to leave Starr Gate for the run north. The turning circle track is chaired, with wood ties. (11.5.49)

BOURNEMOUTH

Above: Trolleybus No 142 built in 1935 is seen at The Square, hub of the system. It is smartly decked out in primrose yellow and maroon, with town crests on both decks. The complex Square layout provided a series of laybys, letting each group of routes load without delaying others. Construction and comfort of the trolleybuses was above average. The high load factor throughout the day justified extravagant rear entrance and front exit with separate stairs. The 3-axle double deckers had only 56 seats against 70 on a lighter London trolleybus of equal size. (9.8.53)

Right: To avoid inconvenience of turning buses to return on the same routes, some routes were linked at the outer ends. No 287 has come from The Square on route 23 via Cromleigh Avenue and will return via Southbourne on route 22. This was one of the last new British trolleybuses. It is of 1959 design.

Above: Standard prewar trolleybus was a 3-axle Sunbeam with Park Royal body. No 141 built in 1935 is seen at Winton bound for Square. Such trolleybuses replaced opentop trams like those sold to Llandudno. Sunbeams ran during World War 2 in London, Newcastle and Wolverhampton. (9.8.53)

Right: Narrow Tuckton Bridge had portal framework for trolleybus overhead. Weight limitations meant trolleybuses were restricted to 10mph on the bridge, and only one was allowed to cross at once. The trolleybus is one of the 1959 batch. (23.9.67)

Above left: Seen at Christchurch after leaving the turntable, No 302 was the last but one trolleybus built for Bournemouth or any British system. It made its debut in October 1962. Modern techniques enabled the front platform to be located before the front wheels. Seating capacity was increased to 65 even with two stairways. The Christchurch group of routes lasted to the end. But by 1969 no other system wanted modern trolleybuses. (23.9.67)

Above: At Christchurch terminus the trolleybus ran onto the turntable in foreground. The trolleypoles were lowered and fixed. The bus was pushed through 180°, and driven off after rewirement of trolleypoles. This view of No 280 shows that the 1959 trolleybuses had the same rear aspect as older vehicles. (23.9.67)

Left: Wiring had to be provided on some roads for depot access without lengthy detouring. These links weren't used often, and then mainly in one direction at certain times. This link to Southcote Road depot is a rare case of 'single line' trolleybus wiring. Buses shared the same positive wire both ways. (9.8.53)

BRIGHTON

Left: Corporation trolleybus No 42 was built by AEC in 1939 to replace open top trams that ceased to operate just before World War 2 started. It pauses at Hollingbury before completing the circle back to Aquarium. Brighton, Hove & District was unique in the Tilling group in owning and operating trolleybuses in conjunction with a municipality. Besides the fleet number, Corporation vehicles could be spotted by the large wheel hubs and town crest on the sides. Despite imminent closure, No 42 is still smart and well maintained. The Hollingbury circle was the last section to open. Brighton trolleybuses ceased to run in 1961. (6.10.59)

CLEETHORPES

Left: This unusual maroon and white Grimsby trolleybus turns at Cleethorpes on the joint service between both towns. The Grimsby and Cleethorpes systems merged in 1957 and closed in 1960. (23.9.52)

DERBY

Right: Trolleybuses formed the
backbone of city transport in Derby
from the early 1930s to the early
1960s. On the last day of
trolleybuses, Sunbeam type F4 with
8ft-wide Brush body lays over at
Midland Station. It is on circuitous
route 33 from Market Place via
Cavendish. (9.9.67)

DUNDEE

Left: Dundee's newest cars were assigned to the Lochee line, where a 1930-vintage car is about to leave the leafy terminus for Reform Street. Despite their dated look the cars were comfortable and smoothriding. (22.7.52)

Above: Lookalike applegreen and cream cars with bumper stickers throng Dundee's High Street. At left is curbside loading for Downfield and Maryfield cars. The efficient network closed two years after this photo was taken. (17.6.54)

Right: Dundee car No 9 lays over at Blackness before leaving for Downfield. The spruce applegreen and cream paintwork has full striping. Dundee possessed no modern cars, but all plant was well maintained. (22.7.52)

EDINBURGH

Left: Late Saturday afternoon crowds thronging Leith Street aren't overly interested in the passing cars. Yet in little over two years the last line will close. Standard car No 216, built at Shrubhill shops in 1939, is bound from Fairmilehead to Stanley Road. (12.6.54)

Bottom left: An inbound car nears gauntleted track at Musselburgh Town Hall soon after leaving Levenhall, five months before the line closed. The Joppa-Levenhall line was the only outcity part of the network. Car No 161 was built at Shrubhill shops in 1931. (12.6.54)

Above right: Experimental car No 180 built at Shrubhill shops in 1932 is seen at Granton South terminus on the Firth of Forth. Car No 180 had a composite frame, metal cladding, and bulkhead-free upper deck. The wide valance over upper deck windows gave it an apart look. Features from 180 were incorporated in the new Standards, like that on the right. (3.6.52)

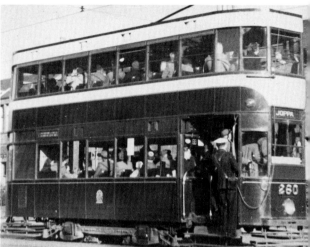

Centre right: Car No 260 built by Metropolitan Cammell in 1933 passes Zoo Park bound for Joppa, soon after leaving Corstorphine. Buses replaced Corstorphine routes two years later, but 260 ran until 1956. (1.6.52)

Below: Monumental Tollcross depot, the last shed in use, was built in 1897 as a cable powerhouse. Off-service Standard No 180 was built in 1936 at Shrubhill shops. (5.6.52)

Left: The last part of the
Corstorphine line, opened 1937, was
the final Edinburgh extension. Metal
plates on the overhead were
introduced in 1940 to help crews
find the wire at night. Car No 12 was
built in 1935 by Hurst Nelson.
(3.8.51)

Below left: After turning the
trolleyarm the conductor reboards at
Corstorphine for the return to
Liberton. The still rural setting has a
fine mountain backdrop. Standard
car No 40 was built in 1937 in
Shrubhill shops. (5.6.52)

Right: Late in the afternoon
Standard car No 93 built in 1923 by
Leeds Forge Co lays over at Granton
Road station. It is bound for
Morningside station where there is a
spur off the main line. This route
lasted until the system closed in
1956. (23.7.52)

Below: At Churchill a route 5 car
nears Morningside station on its run
from Piershill. Standard car No 118
was built in 1931 at Shrubhill shops.
(6.6.52)

GLASGOW

Above: Scuffed dash and plunging windshield stress the age of Glasgow Standard No 226 built in 1914. It is about to leave Arden for University. Route 14 mixed old and new cars. (15.6.57)

Right: Coronation car No 1254 built in 1937 enters Dennistoun shed. Glasgow built 150 of these fine cars in its Coplawhill shops. Restrictive curves meant that despite end tapering and limited length, Coronations couldn't be used on all lines. The lower deck was orange, the upper applegreen, and roof and window frames cream. (2.6.52)

Left: Glasgow's Cunarders were the largest batch of cars built for a British system after World War 2. From 1948-52 101 modernised Coronations left Coplawhill shops. These very advanced cars had a luxurious interior, but unstable riding on inside bearing axles was never cured. Here No 1333 shows its fine lines on route 8 at Rouken Glen just after entering service. The last Cunarders ran in 1962, when the system closed. (-.9.49)

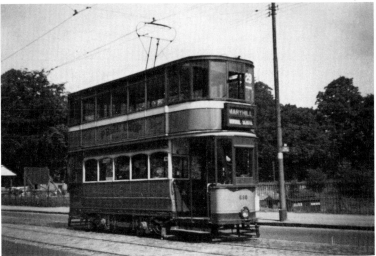

Centre left: Standard No 660 built in 1902 is about to leave Uddingston for Maryhill. Older cars were brightly painted, with applegreen sides up and orange down. Upperdeck window frames were brown, lower cream, and trucks maroon. Some veterans ran 60 years, after rebuilding for increased comfort and speed. (14.6.54)

Below: Standard No 582, built 1902, halts on Bilsland Drive Maryhill, bound for Springburn. Standard cars gave up to 60 years service. Despite antiquated looks they were fast and rode well on Glasgow's good track. (19.6.57)

Top right: Experimental single-truck car No 1001 was built in 1940 at Coplawhill shops. The car was patterned on the Coronations with large windows, luxurious seating, roof lights, and wide entrances, features often lacking in modern buses. (4.6.52)

Centre right: A route 14 car stands at rural Barrhead terminus before leaving for University. The line once ran through to Paisley. Cunarder No 1389 was one of 101 built in 1948-52. They were the last British cars built in quantity and the only double-deckers with resilient wheels and inside-frame trucks. Standards and Cunarders were mixed on route 14. (30.7.52)

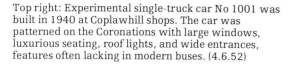

Below: Glasgow trolleybus TD2 is seen at Hampden Park openair lot. One trolleybus was loaned to Edinburgh for trials. Never an important feature of Glasgow's transport, trolleybuses ran from 1949 to 1967. (-.6.57)

HASTINGS

Left and below: Restored 1928 Guy opentop trolleybus with Dodson body has just returned to service. It is running a special seafront service at normal fares. At night it is illuminated by rainbow lamps fed from the traction supply. The system opened in 1928 with 58 trolleybuses eight of which were open top. Gantry-mounted trolleyarms were liable to rain grease on passengers. After 1935 brown and cream gave way to the green and cream of Maidstone & District that had bought the system. (19.8.53)

Left: The green and white trolleybuses bore the title Hastings Tramways Company until about 1957. Here No 39 lays over at Ore, a typical hilly route for which the vehicles were so suited. Hastings trolleybuses ran from 1928-1959. (-.8.50)

Below: Hastings Old Town High Street was too narrow for trolleybuses to pass. No 20 nears Memorial on its run from Ore to Silverhill. (25.3.56)

Right: Sunbeam trolleybus No 31, built 1947, passes Bull Inn Bulverhythe turning circle. This section of new trolleybus route avoided a former tramway right-of-way. No 31 was one of the last new 25 trolleybuses delivered 1945-47. The route through Hastings and Bexhill to Cooden was a rare example of trolleybuses running in part on the seafront, but service was infrequent. (19.8.53)

Below right: Trolleybuses Nos 11 and 19 of a 20-vehicle batch built by AEC in 1940 lay over at Ore. They were of normal construction and layout, and gave a quiet, smooth ride. No 19 is about to leave for Silverhill. (11.7.54)

Above: Regular services ran from Silverhill depot. From right to left are trolleybuses Nos 42, 23, and repainted No 6. Bulverhythe shed served for storage and as a works. (25.3.56)

Centre right: This view of Silverhill depot looks toward the west entrance and shows trolleybuses Nos 23 and 42. The 3ft 6in gauge tram track is still in place after 27 years disuse. Rails are bolted foot to foot for extra strength over service pits. (25.3.56)

Below right: Hastings trolleybus No 35 lays over on the Ridge at St Helens before returning to Hollington via Old Town. The large area of white sets off the green of this neat design. (30.3.56)

HELLINGLY

Left: This green Hellingly Hospital Railway locomotive takes power by trolley-pole from an overhead wire at Hellingly station on Southern Region. In passenger days there was a between-tracks platform. The line opened 1899 to link a large hospital with the London, Brighton & South Coast Railway between Eridge and Polegate. It was electrified in 1903. A passenger service was worked by a tramway-like car, and a two-axle locomotive looked after freight traffic. Passenger service ceased in 1931 but freight held up until the late 1950s. It was one of the few light railways in the south of England. (10.5.52)

HUDDERSFIELD

Left: Huddersfield's smart red and cream trolleybus No 502 stands over at Lindley before heading east to Waterloo. The trolleybuses ran from 1933 until 1968. (22.9.50)

IPSWICH

Above: Trolleybus No 115 at Felixstowe Road Priory Heath is about to leave for Electric House, main city terminus. Notable are the tiny destination box and mottled aluminium side panels. (15.4.61)

Right: Sunbeam trolleybus No 126 of 1950, seen at Whitton, was the last built for Ipswich. In 1962 it was sold to Walsall, where it ran until 1970. Ipswich trolleybuses were referred to as trams in public notices. The system started in 1923 and was extended until 1949. The last trolleybus ran in 1963. (15.4.61)

LEEDS

Left: Soon after entering Leeds service Feltham No 527, built in 1931, halts on City Square bound for Halton. Leeds bought 90 Felthams displaced by London closures. They ran mainly on York Road right-of-way lines. Behind is a Chamberlain car on the Roundhay Circular. (4.6.51)

Below: Car No 276 heads Transport across imposing City Square. This neat product of the Leeds City transport workshops was the first new post-World War 2 car and entered service in 1948. A serious shortage was met by buying secondhand cars. (18.9.54)

Above: A Circular Route 3 car on New Briggate at Vicar Lane heads north to Roundhay and Chapeltown. Horsfield car No 216 is painted light blue. (9.6.51)

Centre right: Chamberlain car No 99 waits for an ex-Southampton domed roof car to reverse at Moortown. On the right is a Horsfield car. The Chamberlain is dark blue, the others being light blue. (4.6.51)

Below right: Whingate terminus was located in a pleasant area of redbrick houses. Feltham No 505, built in 1931, carries a tryout paint scheme. It's about to leave on the long crosstown run east to Crossgates. (4.6.51)

Left: Car No 265 at Middleton is one of 17 built in 1933-35 for the line. These solid, heavy cars rode best on the wooded right-of-way. The Middleton Circle was completed in 1949 by the last extension, from Belle Isle to Middleton. The cars were withdrawn in 1959 when the line closed. (8.6.51)

Centre left: A Horsfield car speeds south from Lawnswood along Otley Road to central Leeds. Well-sited right-of-way enabled towering trees to be preserved, and the line doesn't disturb highclass living areas. The Horsfield was a revamped traditional type with folding doors, but the top end windows, normally a prime viewpoint, were blocked by indicators. Some Horsfields ran until the system closed in 1959. (16.9.54)

Below: Light blue car No 277 at Headingley depot was built for London in 1930 as HR/2 No 1881. It was one of three HR/2s sold to Leeds in 1939. (4.6.51)

LIVERPOOL

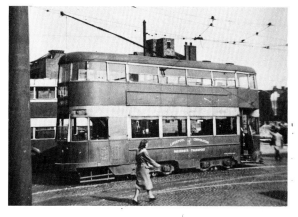

Left: Ten days before route 10 closed, a Prescot-bound car lays over at South Castle Street in central Liverpool. Route 10 had much right-of-way. Car No 800 dates to the mid-1930s and was forerunner of 270 streamliners. (9.5.49)

Centre left: A conductor leaves his streamliner at Liverpool's busy Pierhead. There were three turning circles at this main central area terminus. Many people transferred between cars and ferries. (9.5.49)

Below: Old Liverpool single-truck car No 747 contrasts with modern housing and road layout at Page Moss Avenue as it curves back to Pierhead. The horizontal catenary overhead is a study in itself. (1.10.51)

Right: A Liverpool single-truck car waits at Page Moss Avenue before leaving for Pierhead. Over 100 cars of this 1938 type were built, the largest British fleet of single truck streamliners. They were the last to run when the system closed in 1957. (1.10.51)

Below right: Car No 154 prepares to leave Bowring Park for Pierhead 15 months before final closure. No 154 was one of 150 streamliners built at Edge Lane shops in 1936-37. Many developed body defects after only 15 years and had to be rebuilt. Some saw further service in Glasgow. (16.6.56)

LLANDUDNO

Above: Llandudno & Colwyn Bay car No 7 heads inland at Rhos as it nears Colwyn Bay only six months before closure. No 7 was built in 1925 for Bournemouth to an obsolete design, and came to Llandudno in 1936. Although the scenic line was a big tourist draw, local councils refused to fund operations. (27.8.55)

Left: The Llandudno & Colwyn Bay line ran next to the sea for a short way only, at Rhos. Ex-Accrington car No 3 was built about 1920 and regauged from 4ft to 3ft 6in for Llandudno. Rhos Pier is behind the car as it heads inland toward Colwyn Bay. (5.10.51)

Left: Just west of Rhos was the Llandudno & Colwyn Bay depot. Car Nos 17 and 18 alone survived of the 1907 fleet. They were typical interurbans with wideapart equal-wheel trucks, but two of the four motors were later removed. The cars have two trolleyarms and bodyarching shows their age. (30.9.51)

Centre left: Llandudno-bound car No 12 skirts the rocky shore at Penrhyn Bay. The Little Orme forms a rugged backdrop. Car No 12 was built in 1925 for Bournemouth and came to the line in 1936. (30.9.51)

Below: Llandudno & Colwyn Bay car No 24 was one of two bought from Darwen in 1946. Built in 1937, these were the only British narrow-gauge streamliners. They were assigned to the Colwyn Bay-Rhos run and contrasted grotesquely with the oldtimers. The exposed shore at Penrhyn prevented through running to Llandudno. (5.10.51)

Above: Passengers enjoy an opentop ride in the last summer of the Llandudno & Colwyn Bay line. Car No 10 was built for Bournemouth in 1921 and sold to Llandudno in 1936. It is on unmade Glan-y-Mor Road near Little Orme, Llandudno-bound. The line crammed varied scenery into its seven miles, with street and right-of-way running. (27.8.55)

Left: Ex-Darwen car No 24 at Rhos depot prepares to return to Colwyn Bay. (5.10.51)

Below: A veteran of 1907 prepares to leave Llandudno's West Shore. Only two of the 14 cars were left by 1951. They had 42 lengthwise seats with smoking and nonsmoking sections. (5.10.51)

Above: Britain's only cablecars climb from Llandudno to near Great Orme Summit. Passengers transfer halfway as the line is in two parts. Here car No 4 climbs a 20% grade on a lower street section. Little Orme is visible across Llandudno Bay. (5.10.51)

Below: The Great Orme Railway's dark blue, windowless car No 7 at Summit terminus carries trolleypoles for telephone contact with the power house. The upper section cable is exposed between unpaved rails. (5.10.51)

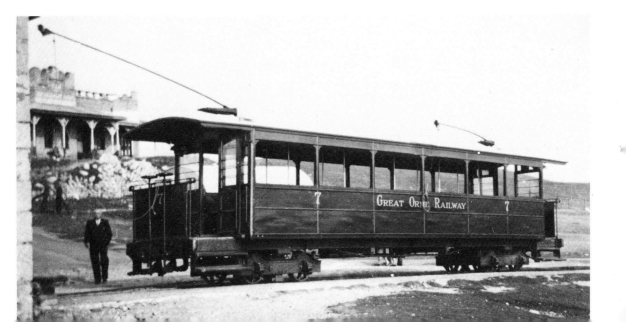

LONDON

Right: E/3 No 1956 is about to leave Manor House for West Norwood. Before route 33 closed in April 1952, car No 1956 ran from Norwood Depot. It was one of 100 built in 1930-31 for the Kingsway Tunnel routes. E/3s were similar to E/1s, but metal-bodied. The interior was brightened, roller-bearing axleboxes fitted, and stencil route numbers introduced. The route box slide showed it was a Tunnel car, but destinations lighted from the front were harder to read than on older cars. (20.1.52)

Below: At Manor House terminus E/3s No 1946 from Holloway depot and No 1993 from Norwood depot are juxtaposed. They belong to a group of 100 built in 1930-31. Until 1938 there was a changepit at Manor House. The chain across the platform of No 1946 shows it is off service. (-.4.51)

Above: Kingsway Subway's Holborn station gave convenient transfer to the Underground. The sign is partly blanked out as route 31 ceased in September 1950. Kingsway still has powerful gaslamps that can be heard hissing at nights on Subway platforms. The corner clock shows Subway cars still have 12 hours to run on this last day. Scrapping of this subsurface Embankment to Bloomsbury link aroused little opposition. (5.4.52)

Left: On the last morning of Kingsway Subway service, E/3 No 1993, built 1931, tops Bloomsbury ramp as an LT man unconcernedly rolls a cigarette. Cars entering Theobalds Road tripped a slot contact giving the green to a following car at Holborn station. Bloomsbury was only five minutes ride from Charing Cross. (5.4.52)

Above: A week before final closure, E/3 No 1945 built in 1930 has just reversed at Savoy Street on the Embankment. It is bound for Beresford Square, Woolwich. Cars also turned regularly on the Embankment at Blackfriars, and sometimes at Westminster. The continuous stream of cars however mostly used the Embankment as a loop in both directions with no layover. (26.6.52)

Left: One of London's newest cars, ex-Walthamstow No 2060 built in 1932, lays over at Savoy Street at Saturday midday soon after this type first ran on route 22. The car bears a specially-cut route number. (23.7.49)

Below: Victoria Embankment tracks shaded by lofty planes are seen from atop a car at Charing Cross. The stop sign is of 1949 pattern. In the middle background is Shell Mex Building, and at right the mansard-roofed Strand Hotel, its windows shaded by blinds against the noonday sun. Beyond these buildings the route 33 E/3 ahead will enter Kingsway Tunnel under Waterloo Bridge on its way to Manor House. (-.6.50)

Left: A route 72 car halts on the leafy Embankment at Westminster passenger shelter. It is the last day of the London system. E/3 No 1914 built in 1930 runs late and will turn short of Woolwich at Eltham. Embankment tracks were laid next the river and in effect formed London's only right-of-way. From 1950 the tracks were also shared by buses. Many cars had two trolleyarms to ease changeover from conduit to overhead. The arm was usually secured to a nearside hook at each end. (5.7.52)

Below: Ex-London United Feltham No 2158 built in 1931, at Westminster loading island, is Purley-bound via Blackfriars Bridge five days before Croydon lines closed. Its damaged state hints at a collision with the rear of a truck. (2.4.51)

Right: A route 31 car at Westminster is about to run onto Westminster Bridge bound for Wandsworth High Street. In two weeks this route will be replaced by buses, and E/3 No 1960 in 1931 transferred from Wandsworth Depot to New Cross. (17.9.50)

Below right: Feltham No 2143 built in 1931 descends from Albert Embankment past Lambeth Palace in wan winter sunshine. It nears Savoy Street on a route 22 Saturday midday turn one week before buses took over. Use of Felthams on the 22s was shortlived. St Thomas Hospital and its Campanile Tower appear in the left distance through winter murk typical of this era. (30.12.50)

Above: At Waterloo station's Westminster Bridge Road entrance trolleyless HR/2 No 135 built in 1931 races a Chesham-bound Green Line to Westminster Bridge. It is a Saturday afternoon four weeks before buses replace route 56. The 1936 signalbox controls all Waterloo train movements. (8.9.51)

Right: On Kennington Lane, weatherworn E/1 No 1495, built in 1911, waits for the lights. This car retains original bodywork but the wooden seats have been replaced by upholstery. From 1907-22, 1,000 cars of this type were built. All four corners of Lambeth Road intersection were razed in World War 2. The capped spire of Christchurch is in the left distance. (3.4.51)

Above: Around 1950 loose rail joints on Kennington Road were a problem and forced drivers to slow or risk tripping lifeguards. E/3 No 164 built in 1931 passes track repairs at Fitzalan Street. The route 16 car is bound for Embankment via Westminster Bridge. Georgian houses on the right indicate a onetime fashionable area. (18.2.51)

Right: In bright winter sunshine a man scurries across Brixton Road at the Oval before an oncoming 33 to West Norwood, two months to closure of the Kingsway Tunnel. Beside E/3 No 2002 built in 1931, backed by Kennington Park, is a 109 bus that replaced Croydon cars 10 months before. (9.2.52)

Above: Immaculate HR/2 No 159 waits at Oval station lights on its 10-mile run from Victoria to Blackwall Tunnel. So recently has it left Charlton shops that topdeck ads are still missing. Roundtopped cabs and trolleyless roof enhance this 1931 car, last of a 59-car order. The cab window running number by the stairs shows at least 26 cars served route 58 Sundays. (4.3.51)

Right: This route 33 E/3 south of Blackfriars Bridge is diverted from its regular run over Westminster while a Festival of Britain footbridge is built at Charing Cross. The line branches right along Southwark Street to London Bridge, only section without Sunday service. In the distance is Unilever Building. (16.7.50)

Above: E/1 No 1422 built in 1910 and modernised in 1936, is about to leave Southwark Bridge for Tooting. During 1935-37, about 150 E/1s were rebuilt with revamped interior, cleaned-up exterior, and windshields. (14.8.49)

Left: A route 46 car passes a new block as it heads for Beresford Square Woolwich. Scene is Great Dover Street at Trinity Street 11 weeks before final closure. (20.4.52)

Above: Just after leaving London Bridge for Wandsworth High Street, E/3 No 1928 built in 1930 heads along Southwark Bridge Road at Marshalsea Road. The 19th century street has a World War 2 bomb gap on the right. Four weeks later buses replaced route 12 and trolleybus route 612, restoring the London Bridge to Mitcham facility after 13 years. (2.9.50)

Below: On the east side of Vauxhall oneway scheme a route 12 car halts, to collect Wandsworth-bound passengers, two weeks before closure. The tracks here were remodelled in 1938. A route 2 STL of 1935 vintage overtakes E/3 No 204 built in 1931. On the left is the Waterloo main line viaduct. (17.9.50)

Above: This route 12 car at Princes Head nears the end of its run to Wandsworth High Street two days before buses took over. The tracks on the right lead to Clapham Junction. On the island, smartly dressed controllers ensure a regular service. (28.9.50)

Left: Wandsworth High Street terminus resulted from a cutback of services in 1937, but it was 13 years before the rest of route 12 closed. Meantime route 31 was re-extended from Princes Head to Wandsworth High Street. E/3 No1964 built in 1930 prepares to leave for Agricultural Hall Islington four weeks before closure. (5.9.50)

Top: On Wandsworth Road at Allen Edwards Road, a four-man gang carries out repairs two days before the line closes. London Bridge-bound E/1 No 1771 was built in 1922 and modernised in 1937. It was the last E/1 to be rebuilt by Charlton shops. Wandsworth depot rebuilt E/1s were among the first cars scrapped. (28.9.50)

Above: At the foot of Lavender Hill, route 28 E/1 No 1824 built 1922 runs into Clapham Junction terminus. Behind are route 34 cars. That on the right heads for Battersea Bridge, the other has left Falcon Road, Blackfriars-bound. Arding & Hobbs store is on the right. Route 28 has ended here since 1937, but now it is five days to closure of local routes. (25.9.50)

Left: At Clapham Junction route 26 E/1 No 1671, built in 1912, waits to enter the terminal track before returning to Blackfriars. About half London's cars were E/1s. Unrebuilt cars like No 1671 kept their 1907 look to the end. Some still had wood slat topdeck seats when the last was scrapped in 1952. (9.10.49)

Below: A special car nears the southbound island at Plough Clapham eight weeks before local routes closed. On the left is a large passenger shelter. E/1 No 1822 built in 1922 has both trolleypoles at the rear. The 1800 series E/1s were assigned to Clapham depot. From January 1951 they ran from New Cross until withdrawal a year later. (11.11.50)

Above: One week before closure of Dog Kennel Hill routes, smart HR/2 No 120, built 1931, passes Brixton station on a fans special. Such trips took in lines not in normal use. Car No 120 had comfortable lower deck bucket seats. The 100 series HR/2s had Hurst Nelson bodies identical with the E/3s. Equal-wheel trucks gave more tractive effort. These trolleyless HR/2s ran until April 1952 on Highgate to Forest Hill route 35, the last all-conduit line. (30.9.51)

Left: Embankment-bound E/3 No 1938 built in 1930 has just taken up its plough at Streatham changepit shortly before the Croydon lines closed. The car stops again as the driver lowers the trolleypole. The car is based on Norwood depot and falsely shows a Kingsway Subway slide. (-.3.51)

Above right: An Embankment-bound route 16 car halts at Streatham changepit to run onto conduit track, two weeks before Croydon lines closed. Spare ploughs are stacked at the hut. Other items of equipment are red flag, brazier, and storm lamp. Ex-Croydon car No 399 was one of 25 built in 1927-28 for the Purley to London service. All except nine months of their life was spent thereon and on the Thornton Heath local. (25.3.51)

Right: Ex-Walthamstow No 2057 stops at Norbury station to take up Croydon-bound Saturday morning shoppers. Built in 1932 to 25 year old designs, this car was one of the last to enter London service. The cars were fast, but noisy and roughriding. A parking ban and passenger island could have solved traffic delay problems. (2.9.50)

Top: Feltham No 2145 built in 1931 heads north to Embankment at Tylecroft Road, Norbury. This car was still in a fair state and a bargain for Leeds at £500. These were the first modern British cars built in quantity and ran from Telford Avenue depot, Streatham. Up to 1950 this depot was stocked with Felthams, ex-Walthamstow cars, and car No 1. It was the only depot where ex-LCC cars were not numerous. The temporary stop sign to the left of the car will remain until buses take over in two weeks. (24.3.51)

Above: Ex-Croydon E/1 No 1379 of 1927 design waits at Thornton Heath High Street to enter the terminus, one year before closure. It was one of four ex-Croydon cars rebuilt in 1936 with tidied-up exterior, redecorated interior, and improved seating and lighting. Performance and riding quality were unchanged as the old equipment was kept. This car once ran from Westminster to Norbury 10min faster than the 35min scheduled. The ex-Croydon cars ran from Thornton Heath Depot. For the last 15 months they ran from Purley depot, when Thornton Heath was demolished to build a bus garage. Apart from the Woolwich-Eltham route 44, route 42 was the only London local line, and the only one entirely outside the LCC area. It was mainly single and loop, but had a 3-4 minute weekday service. Fare over the branch from Thornton Heath Pond to High Street was 1½d in 1950, in 1980 it was 10p (2/-). (7.4.50)

Above: At South Croydon E/3
No 1939, built in 1930, boards
Purley-bound passengers beside a
new RT bus two days before closure.
Ex-MET Felthams were withdrawn
for sale to Leeds when Wandsworth
lines closed. For the last six months
Norwood Depot E/3s replaced these
cars on the 16/18s. This is why
No 1939 falsely shows a Kingsway
Subway slide. The section south of
Norbury was the only long
post-World War 2 line outside the
LCC area. Croydon track remained in
good condition up to 1951. There
was very much a local atmosphere
on local lines. (5.4.51)

Left: The special hired by Croydon &
Purley Chamber of Commerce waits
in Purley depot yard hours before
Croydon lines closed. Purley depot
had been a store and overhaul shop.
From January 1950 it became a
running shed while Thornton Heath
was demolished to be rebuilt as a bus
garage. E/1 No 839 was built in 1907
and modernised in 1936. It was one
of the oldest cars still running.
(7.4.51)

Right: Ex-Croydon E/1 No 394 waits to enter Purley terminus. Croydon E/1s, taken over by London Transport in 1933, kept to their home lines almost to the end. Most of the 25 cars survived to be transferred from Purley to New Cross depot in 1951. They were withdrawn with all other E/1s in January 1952. (10.7.49)

Below: Fans mill around handsome newly-painted Feltham No 2094 at Purley on a Light Railway Transport League trip. In 1931 one hundred Felthams entered service on west and north London lines. The innovative interior with passenger flow, driver's cab, airbrakes, and platform doors, meant that 18 years later they were still modern. Felthams were withdrawn when Croydon lines closed in 1951. But it was still possible to ride a Feltham in Leeds until 1959. (1.5.49)

Above right: A route 78 car bound for West Norwood nears Herne Hill one week before bus replacement. E/3 No 195 was built in 1931. A three-man trackgang on Dulwich Road is tightening joints. Power is drawn by pole from the overhead. This section of line was in use for three months more. (29.12.51)

Right: Spruce E/3 No 1998 built in 1931 pauses at Herne Hill lights soon after leaving West Norwood for Manor House. Brockwell Park main entrance is on the right. The left foreground tracks are disused since route 48 closed in January 1952. Route 33 ceased three weeks after this photo was taken. (16.3.52)

Above: E/3 No 181, built in 1931, heads south on Coldharbour Lane at Loughborough Junction, on a mile-long overhead section of an otherwise all-conduit route 34. The 34s turn at Battersea Bridge since it was hit by a collier six months ago, forcing closure of Kings Road Chelsea terminus. Two regulators stand by a billboard advertising Tommy Trinder's Palladium spot. The 48 car at left nears Camberwell changepit. (18.9.50)

Right: Four weeks before bus replacement, a route 58 car bound for Blackwall Tunnel nears Camberwell Green stop. HR/2 No 105 was built in 1931. (9.9.51)

Above: Once-busy Camberwell Green junction is now used by routes 40 and 72 only. Rails branching right to Denmark Hill are tarred over. E/3 No 2002, built 1931, heads for Woolwich Perrott Street within two months of final closure. (17.5.52)

Left: Cars often ran fast on the quiet section of route 58 between Camberwell and Lewisham. Here trolleyless HR/2 No 151 built in 1931 is seen at Camberwell Green bound for Victoria. This type last ran in April 1952, as the remaining lines all called for cars with trolleypoles. (2.4.50)

Above: At Camberwell Green E/1 No 1566 shows off its new paint to Saturday shoppers. This car was built in 1912 and was one of the first to be modernised in 1935 with improved interior and revamped exterior. Modernisation improved end window visibility by relocating the route number. Unrebuilt E/1 No 1005 rounds a curve in pursuit past a fine Victorian store parade. Car No 1566 heads for Savoy Street and No 1005 for Victoria. (3.6.50)

Left: The sylvan peace of Peckham Rye two months before closure is marred only by ugly billboards. The HR/2 built in 1930 was damaged in World War 2 and rebuilt with a top deck like a modernised E/1. (29.7.51)

Above right: Two weeks before buses took over route 58, HR/2 No 1861 built in 1930 passes the Plough Inn Dulwich bound for Blackwall Tunnel. (23.9.51)

Right: Three weeks before closure a route 35 car turns from Stanstead Road into Sunderland Road near Forest Hill terminus. Behind spruce E/3 No 176 built in 1931 and assigned to Holloway depot are signs of World War 2 damage. (15.3.52)

Above left: A route 35 E/3 halts at Cranston Road, Brockley lights near the end of its 14½-mile, Manor House to Forest Hill run. It is three weeks to closure of London's longest post-World War 2 route. Tracks to Blackwall Tunnel and Grove Park on right have been disused three months. (15.3.52)

Left: HR/2 No 1880 built in 1930 halts at Lewisham Town Hall on the Rushey Green triangular junction. Devious route 58 from Blackwall Tunnel to Victoria via Dulwich was replaced six weeks later by buses. (28.8.51)

Above: Wintry sunshine glints on two E/3s passing newly-cleaned Lewisham Clock Tower. The car at left heads for Victoria, that at right for Grove Park. Route 54 was famed for fast runs. On this last Sunday it is but six days to closure. (30.12.51)

Right: On Queens Road at York Grove E/3 No 1974 built in 1930 heads for Savoy Street. The winding, busy road is fronted by fine old houses and large trees like the giant lime on right, as the last high summer of London's cars nears. (17.5.52)

Top: A conductor due for relief leaves his route 74 rebuilt E/1 at New Cross on a Sunday afternoon as a line of cars begins to form. Following E/1 No 565 was built in 1930 with wood lower deck and metal E/3 topdeck. Behind is a rebuilt E/1, and at rear a 1922 E/1. (1.4.51)

Above: Five weeks before final closure, a Sunday shortworking 72 prepares to leave New Cross Gate for Beresford Square Woolwich. HR/2 No 1856, built 1930, is smart but lacks side route numbers and boards. (25.5.52)

Left: On a late Sunday afternoon E/1 No 1817 halts at New Cross near London's largest depot. It came to New Cross three months ago from Clapham. Strapping on both decks guarantees nine months more service. Following E/1 No 1619, built in 1910 and 12 years older, was rebuilt about 1936. Despite the ending of fuel restriction in 1950 there's little traffic. The fine house at left is typical of rundown local properties. (1.4.51)

Below: E/3 No 1949 built in 1930 threads Shardeloes Road near Lewisham Way between lookalike Victorian houses. The street is pleasantly free of waiting vehicles as the 74 heads for Blackfriars two months before the route closed. (11.11.51)

Right: The last mile of the Grove Park line was on the overhead system, serving a modern estate on a road wide enough for right-of-way. Just before Southend changepit, E/3 No 1923, built in 1930, halts as the trolleyarm is raised. At the changepit by the gaslamp, the plough shoots out of the carrier. Wintry sunshine illuminates a scene that four weeks later had gone for ever. (9.12.51)

Below: Cars changed to overhead at Lee Green, a short way before the changepit. Car No 1863 built in 1930 is about to leave the busy intersection, where its trolleyarm has just been raised. It has a Last Tram Week poster on the top deck. (28.6.52)

Above: At Eltham Church ex-East Ham No 93 built in 1928 nears Middle Park Avenue terminus on route 44 from Beresford Square Woolwich. This route and the 42s were the only post-World War 2 local runs. Car 93 had tinted glass lower deck ventilators. Final closedown of the system is one week away. (28.6.52)

Below: Ex-West Ham No 341 built by Brush in 1925 stops at Eltham Church on the last day. West Ham had a large system with through running to adjoining networks. In the 1920s it built many such cars for lines from Aldgate to Ilford and Barking. These closed during 1939 and 1940. Many cars saw use in South London. Eltham area lines were some of the last built by the LCC. Despite wide roads, no attempt was made to modernise track layout. A large variety of cars running from New Cross and Abbey Wood Depots was seen in the area. (5.7.52)

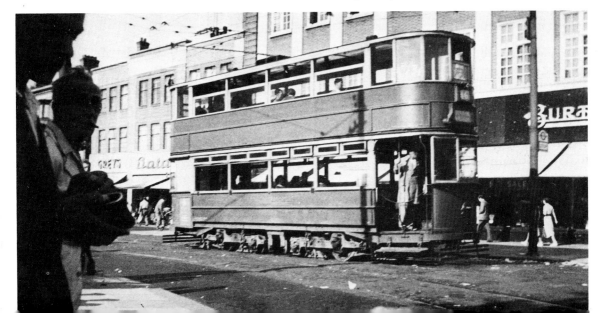

Left: Passengers board car No 2 bound from Southwark Bridge to Woolwich on the last afternoon of operation. Absence of a passenger island on Well Hall Road hinders traffic. Several cars were rebuilt to resemble luxury ex-LCC car No 1 after London Transport took over. Car No 2 was formerly collision-damaged E/1 No 1370. It was thoroughly rebuilt with superior seating, lighting, and inside decor as a model for quantity reconstruction of E/1 and ex-Croydon cars. But rebuilt E/1s didn't have inward-leaning topdeck pillars or domed roof. (5.7.52)

Below: This route 46 car has just passed under Well Hall rail bridge one week before the system closed. Ex-West Ham No 337, built 1925, was stored at Hampstead between 1940-46, after closure of the Aldgate to Barking line. A topdeck front sash window was a feature of this type. (28.6.52)

Right: New Cross-bound E/3 No 1913 built in 1930 pauses at Well Hall Circus to be switched to Westhorne Avenue, in 1932 London's last new trackage. Scuffed dash and soiled blind hint that closure of the system is but three weeks away. Part of Progress Estate is behind the car. At Progress Hall, fans held meetings during 1950-52 in a bid to have the cars retained. (17.6.52)

Below right: On the last day, E/1 No 593 built in 1930 crosses Well Hall Circus on its Woolwich to Eltham run. It is covered with slogans, some doubting the wisdom of scrapping. The 500 series E/1s had new bodies on frames and trucks of scrapped G class cars. The top deck was of E/3 type. The foreground track leads into Westhorne Avenue, London's last new line. Although Eltham lines ran along wide roads, no attempt was made to incorporate right-of-way or passenger islands. (5.7.52)

Above: In the evening peak E/3 No 1929 built in 1930 climbs the oneway Woolwich New Road soon after leaving Beresford Square for Southwark Bridge. It is barely three weeks to final shutdown of the system. Despite increased traffic, bicycles are still part of the scene. (17.6.52)

Left: Beresford Square marketplace was busy Saturdays, but empty in this Sunday shot, save for a 46 due to leave for Southwark Bridge. E/1 No 1608 was built in 1912 and modernised about 1936. Behind is Woolwich Arsenal (14.8.49)

Above right: A No 70 bound for London Bridge waits at quiet Greenwich Church terminus for Sunday passengers. The peace here is now shattered by roaring oneway traffic. E/1 No 840 built in 1907 and often ran on the 68s and 70s. These routes closed three months later. (8.4.51)

Right: As E/3 No 1969 built in 1931 speeds along Woolwich Road at Westcombe Hill bound for Savoy Street, London's cars have but three weeks to run. A 500 series E/1 to Abbey Wood is framed by the bridge carrying the Angerstein Wharf branch. Beyond the left abutment is Charlton Overhaul Shops. (15.6.52)

Right: Ex-West Ham No 330, built in 1932, stands in front of Charlton shops. Three such cars were used for staff runs after World War 2. This type was windshielded from the start, long before LCC cars had driver protection. Open fronted cars ran in London until 1940. (15.8.50)

Below: Soon after leaving Blackwall Tunnel for Victoria, a 58 car turns from Tunnel Avenue into Woolwich Road Greenwich. HR/2 No 105 was built in 1931. Just visible behind it is a Tunnel STL bus. (12.8.51)

Above: By Blackwall Lane gasholder, HR/2 No 1871 built in 1930 waits to enter the terminus, badly sited in mid-highway near the Tunnel ramp. Running number 24 in the cab window shows the Sunday interval was about 6min. Route 58 closed down four months later. (20.5.51)

Left: On a quiet Sunday morning HR/2 No 1854 is about to leave Blackwall Tunnel for Victoria. This car was one of 50 built in 1930 with equal-wheel trucks and all axles motored for hilly lines. Forest Hill to Camberwell was the hilliest and pleasantest run on the post-World War 2 London system. (12.6.49)

Below: From the eastbound track on Woolwich Road Charlton a branch is being built to Penhall Road Scrapyard. The conduit slot already deviates to the left rail to end at a changepit just inside the yard, as storage tracks had overhead wires. (29.1.50)

Top: Partially wrecked E/1 No 1260 sits among reclaimed wheelsets at Penhall Road awaiting its fate. It was built in 1910 and the top deck was modernised after an accident. This view was taken four weeks before first route closures. (6.9.50)

Above: Penhall Road Scrapyard opened summer 1950 for condemned cars. Salvagable fittings have been taken from the car on the left. It will be tipped from its trucks and burnt, the fate of most London cars excepting Felthams. These cars are E/1s, with a work car at right. It is but two weeks before the first influx of cars displaced by buses. (19.9.50)

Above: Fifty-eight cars awaited scrapping at Penhall Road after Battersea and Wandsworth lines closed in September 1950, the first route cutbacks for a decade. Head cars from left to right are: E/1 No 1770 built 1922, rebuilt 1936; stores car No 05 built 1905; E/1 No 1170 built 1909; E/1 No 1645 built 1912, rebuilt about 1936. (1.10.50)

Centre left: Some of the 40 Felthams withdrawn when Croydon lines closed are seen from the Woolwich Road entrance to Penhall Road scrapyard three days later. The changepit is behind the hut on left. The last Feltham did not leave for Leeds until six months later. They ran there until Leeds closed in 1959. (10.4.51)

Left: At Penhall Road George Cohen processed up to 100 cars every three months by burning wood from metal. This shell was once an E/3 lower deck. Very few cars were museumised though they could have been saved for a song. In the foreground is a magnetic trackbrake assembly. (6-52)

Above: At Royal Hill Greenwich E/3
No 207 built in 1931 heads for Savoy
Street. It has a sandbag on the cab
roof to stop leaks. Cars couldn't
reverse on the single line because of
the double conduit. Vacant lots on
right and in the background stem
from World War 2. (12.8.51)

Right: Two weeks before final
closure, E/3 No 168 built in 1931
descends Woolwich Church Street at
Prospect Vale past Royal Dockyard.
It has just left Woolwich for Savoy
Street. (15.6.52)

Above: At Beresford Square
Woolwich trolleybuses on the
Bexleyheath route pass a late Sunday
afternoon 46 bound for Southwark
Bridge. E/1 No 1836 built in 1922 is
based on New Cross depot since
Clapham routes closed in January.
Isolated from the main system,
Bexley and Dartford trolleybuses
started 1935 and gave way to buses
in 1959. (22.4.51)

Left: A 696 trolleybus to Woolwich
passes a No 38 car to Abbey Wood on
Plumstead High Street two weeks
before the last car ran. Trolleybus
drivers had to be careful not to
overtake the cars, as only one set of
wires was provided for each
direction. The D2 trolleybus was
built in 1936-37, the E/3 car in
1931. (22.6.52)

Above: Two weeks to final closedown, an Embankment-bound E/1 built in 1930 turns from Basildon Road Plumstead into Bostall Hill. The Wickham Lane to Abbey Wood section had extra wires for trolleybuses. Unusually too, the full width of the road is settpaved. (23.6.52)

Right: Car No 2 is about to leave Abbey Wood terminus for Embankment. This car was modernised in 1933 with a domed-roof topdeck and ran until the system closed. Other lookalike cars were Nos 982, 1103, 1260, 1370 and 1444. (17.6.51)

Right: Waterloo signalbox watches over old houses on Addington Street, where children play next to Festival of Britain tracklaying. From a stubend and triangular junction at the distant viaduct a single line extents 400ft to York Road at County Hall. Yokes and slot rails were always laid first. The line is for cars to Oval and Elephant. (25.3.50)

Below: York Road to Addington Street curve assembly at County Hall is complete. Alternate short and long yokes, with ties at long yokes only, support rails and conduit slot. They await concreting and forming of conduit channel. A timber baulk at right foreground helps destress the curve. (25.3.50)

Top: Passers-by seem disinterested in New Street track, where the road is being surfaced. The southbound oneway track ends in an extended yoke, and will connect with Westminster Bridge Road. (9.5.50)

Above: York Road track at County Hall is completed to Westminster Bridge Road where a route 35 E/3 speeds north to Highgate. The conduit bottom is concreted, but the sides must yet be formed and electric T-rails installed. (21.5.50)

Right: Tracklaying begins at Stangate Green with placement of yokes and fastening of slot and running rails. The bolted-on curve checkrail can be seen. Behind is Lambeth Palace Road. This track is for Westminster-bound cars. (21.5.50)

Top: At the County Hall oneway scheme, track on Westminster Bridge Road is being excavated to join New Street curve on right. To the left of the near rail is a subsurface electric T-rail. Part of County Hall is in the background. E/1 No 1579 on route 40 bound for Beresford Square Woolwich was built in 1912 and modernised in 1936. (28.5.50)

Above: E/3 No 1908, built in 1930, threads the S-curve on County Hall oneway tracks from Addington Street to Westminster Bridge Road, only two months before the system closed. The new and expensive tracks had but two years' use. Car No 1908 is still smart and even boasts a clean destination blind for its run to Woolwich Perrott Street. (10.5.52)

Right: On a vacant lot at St Thomas Hospital, London Transport has stockpiled track parts. They are for the south side of the County Hall oneway scheme. These are exciting days for fans, able for the first and last time since 1938 to see new conduit track building. In the background are a double yoke (left) and a single yoke (right) for supporting junction work. (19.7.50)

Below: These children find the County Hall tracklaying site a fine playground. The curved Stangate Green line for Westminster-bound cars is finished. It is being joined to a new track in the background for cars to Vauxhall. Blocks on Lambeth Palace Road were demolished for road widening. (19.7.50)

Above: A 200ft curve sweeps across Stangate Green — at a cost of some trees. It will be used by Westminster-bound cars. Foreground track is being extended for 400ft to the left on Lambeth Palace Road to meet existing track. This was London's last new conduit track. (24.7.50)

Left: Now the north half of the County Hall oneway trackage is in use, work on the south part proceeds. A oneway link is being laid in Lambeth Palace Road for Vauxhall-bound cars. Yokes in the trench await levelling. Behind, the curve to Westminster branches off at left. (24.7.50)

Right: Track at the junction of Lambeth Palace Road and New Curved Street (right) is being concreted. It is for Westminster-bound cars. Junction work was made by Hadfields, Sheffield. Beyond, new track is being laid for cars westbound from Westminster to Vauxhall. (27.7.50)

Below: Lambeth Palace Road track for Vauxhall-bound cars is extended westward. This track had only three months' use. (8.8.50)

Left: Work on the south side of the County Hall oneway scheme nears completion. Track is being excavated so that the new Lambeth Palace Road southbound line can be connected. Rails on concrete blocks are restrained by wood baulks. It's a ticklish job working next to the conduit and energised T-rails. Part of a T-rail and cylindrical insulator appear in the middle foreground. (19.9.50)

Centre left: On the south side of the County Hall oneway tracks, the new Lambeth Palace Road southbound on right is about to be joined to existing track, excavated and temporarily supported. County Hall is in the left background. (7.10.50)

Below: The Westminster Bridge Road to Lambeth Palace Road curve for cars to Westminster nears completion. Two weeks later it was connected, and south side oneway tracks opened. The open foreground track is supported on blocks. (7.10.50)

Above: Moorgate office blocks dwarf
AEC trolleybuses No 1362 of type L1
built in 1939 (front) and No 910 of
Class J1 built in 1938. No 1362 has
runback and coasting brakes for
Highgate Hill. This route was
replaced by buses a year later.
Except for the Farringdon to Grays
Inn Road link on High Holborn,
trolleybuses weren't able to reach
central London. London termini
were awkwardly situated, leading to
duplication between buses and
trolleybuses. (18.7.59)

Right: This trolleybus on Fortess
Road Kentish Town is running off
service to the Monnery Road
entrance of Holloway depot. Buses
took over the 639s in 1961. (2.7.56)

Left: Trolleybus services were so frequent that photos show several vehicles together. At Edgware terminus E1 type No 558 built in 1937 waits to leave for Hammersmith on route 666. Overtaking is C3 type No 304, built in 1936, Barnet-bound on route 645. These routes ran from 1936 to 1962. (18.7.59)

Centre left: Three parallel sets of trolleybus wires smoothed the flow of trolleybuses at North Finchley. Nearing the stop is No 277 of type C2, built 1936, based on Stonebridge and bound for Hammersmith on route 660. At left No 931 of type J1 built in 1938 based on North Finchley is on route 621. As it's Saturday afternoon, No 931 will end at Kings Cross instead of Holborn Circus. (18.7.59)

Below: A large well laid-out terminus was provided at Waltham Cross in Hertfordshire, northern limit of the trolleybus system. In the Saturday midday rushour five are waiting under control of two regulators. Their hut is on the right. On the left is 1541 of Class M1, built 1939, and on the right No 1692 of class K3 built in 1940. (18.7.59)

Above: Two of London's last new
trolleybuses are seen at Wimbledon
Town Hall. Class Q1 Nos 1815 and
1830 built by BUT in 1948 have
120hp motors against 95hp of older
models. Originally the south-west
routes they served were to be kept
until 1970 but closed in 1962 when
all trolleybuses ceased. Spain
showed interest in Q1s, so they were
withdrawn and replaced by older
trolleybuses from closed routes.
No 1815 went to Vigo in 1961 and
No 1830 to Pontevedra in 1960. At
least 20 trolleybuses ordered for
London were diverted to Newcastle.
Similar vehicles were built for
Nottingham. (2.9.53)

Right: B1 class trolleybus No 64,
built 1935, passes the fringe of
Croydon Airport as it heads along
Stafford Road to Crystal Palace. In
1935 the Sutton to Croydon section
opened. It was extended to Crystal
Palace in 1936. The suburbscape is
typical of many London trolleybus
routes. (12.9.54)

Above: Standard D2 trolleybus No 449 with Leyland body built in 1937 leaves West Croydon for Willesden Junction. This trolleybus was one of the few to retain an original half-cab with lengthwise seat up front. Eight of the D2s were destroyed in World War 2. Route 630 opened in 1937 and closed in 1960. (2.9.53)

Below: Leyland B1 class trolleybus No 76 about to leave Crystal Palace for Sutton is fitted with coasting and runback brakes for steep Anerley Hill. B1s were shorter than standard trolleybuses and had 10 less seats. Route 654 was always worked by B1s from Sutton depot, later renamed Carshalton to avoid confusion with a bus garage. The 654s ran through from Crystal Palace to Sutton from 1936 to 1959. (11.4.54)

MAIDSTONE

Above: Maidstone Sunbeam trolleybus No 71 bound for Bull Inn Barming halts at Fountain Inn turning circle near Barming terminus. This was the end of the first 1¾-mile route from Town Hall, opened 1928. No 71 was built in 1947 and scrapped in 1965. It is painted in the current milk chocolate brown. (7.9.53)

Above right: Saturday morning shoppers wait patiently to board a Barming-bound trolleybus on Maidstone's High Street. No 54 was built in 1943 and rebodied in 1960 in utility style. With No 72 it made the last run from Town Hall to Barming Road, 15 April 1967, when the system closed. (-.7.57)

Right: Trolleybus No 56 on Loose Road near Loose has angular utility bodywork and once had wood seats. It ran until the system closed in 1967. The overhead wires are closer together than normal on trolleybus systems. (7.9.53)

ISLE OF MAN

Right: A Manx Electric crossbench set crosses Laxey Viaduct Douglas-bound. At Laxey the line takes a 180° turn to climb the distant hillside to the rocky seashore and Ramsey. (10.6.56)

Centre right: Manx electric 44-seat crossbench trailer No 43 was built by Milnes in 1903. The pulldown blinds are for bad weather protection. (12.6.56)

Below: Snaefell Mountain Railway car No 5 descends against a dramatic mountain backdrop, with conical North Barrule Peak in the middle. The 3ft 6in gauge rack line opened in 1895 and climbs 1,800ft in five miles. Electrical equipment of these veterans was recently modernised by using parts from modern Aachen cars! (10.6.56)

NOTTINGHAM

Above: Smart in a green paint scheme, two trolleybuses to London Q1 design are seen at Bull Market terminus. Nottingham trolleybuses once carried route letters, and later received numbers above those for bus routes. (23.7.62)

Below: This 2-axle Karrier type W trolleybus built in 1945 retains its Park Royal utility bodywork. It is crossing city centre Market Place, hub of the system. Nottingham trolleybuses ran from 1927 to 1966. (23.7.62)

PORTSMOUTH

Below left: Most Portsmouth trolleybuses served the Dockyard. A three-lane layout enabled vehicles to stand without blocking others. Two pre-World War 2 AEC trolleybuses, Nos 298 and 282 (right) wait to leave for Eastney and Copnor Bridge. Behind is a postwar BUT trolleybus. AEC trolleybuses had only 52 seats and the same moquette upholstery as the LNER used for first class seats. (13.5.61)

Right: In September 1955 the Municipal Passenger Transport Association Annual Conference met in Portsmouth. Preference shown for motorbuses over trolleybuses already caused anxiety. Opportunity was taken to demonstrate a modern trolleybus in normal service for one week. Brand new Walsall No 864 was 30ft long and 8ft wide, larger than Portsmouth trolleybuses, thanks to a Ministry of Transport dispensation for 2-axle buses. The Willowbrook body on a Sunbeam chassis seated 36 up and 34 down. Inside layout was traditional but rear-platform doors were power-operated. No 864 is in bright blue paint scheme at Cosham Red Lion, northern limit of the system. However Portsmouth trolleybus scrapping started in 1958, and the last ran in 1963. (1.10.55)

Below: Loaned Walsall trolleybus 864 turns onto the seafront at South Parade Southsea. (1.10.55)

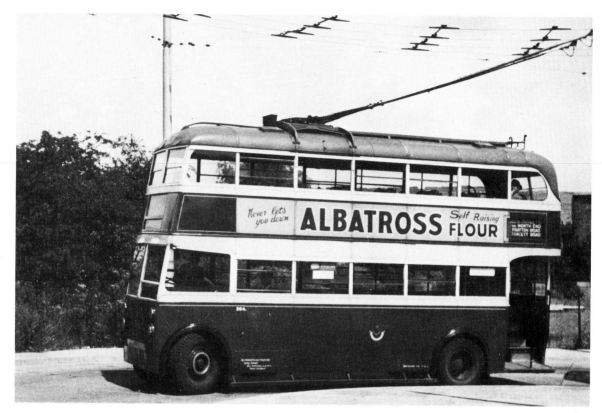

Above: Cosham was an important terminus with a private turning circle. It was located in a yard where until 1924 passengers interchanged between Corporation cars and the Portsdown & Horndean Light Railway. Trolleybus No 264 was built by AEC in 1936. (14.7.53)

Centre left: On Festing Road Southsea BUT trolleybus No 312, built in 1951, heads for the dockyard on the circuitous route from Cosham. Routes had different numbers for each direction. High population density on Portsea Island justified trolleybus operation. (13.7.61)

Below left: No 301 was the first of 15 Burlingham-bodied BUT trolleybuses built in 1951. It is seen on route 13 from Cosham approaching South Parade Pier at Southsea. Here trolleybuses ran along the seafront against a typical hotelscape. (15.7.53)

Above right: Portsmouth's maroon and white trolleybuses were always clean, with oldstyle number and full striping. No 275 built in 1936 with Craven body was one of a 76-vehicle order. It is about to leave well laid out Cosham turning circle for South Parade Pier. (-.9.51)

Right: Portsmouth trolleybuses at Cosham turning circle are No 312 built in 1951 by BUT on left, and No 271 dating to about 1936. Traction poles were painted silver. The system closed between 1958 and 1963. During this time some turns were worked by trolleybuses and some by motorbuses, leaving an indistinct picture (-.3.53)

READING

Right: Smart maroon trolleybus
No 114 built about 1950 nears
Liverpool Road terminus.
Trolleybuses first ran in 1936.
Extensions were opened until 1963,
but the system closed in 1968.
(-.10.52)

SHEFFIELD

Below left: Roberts car No 511 of 1950 design passes Fargate in the central area bound for Eccleshall. (6.6.51)

Above: Near Sheffield's LMR station, car No 452 stops at a crossing. This car was built in 1918 by Cravens. Even then curved glass end windows graced Sheffield cars. Car No 452 boasts striping up and down on its cream and navy blue panels (-.10.52)

Centre right: On Abbey Lane near Beauchief, Standard car No 282 of 1936 design heads north to Lane Top. About 80 of these pleasing single-truck cars were built, their appearance enhanced by cleanness and absence of ads. (21.9.52)

Right: The crewmen of Roberts car No 515 at Eccleshall are proud of their charge. Only 35 were built in 1950-52 but even so it was the largest post-World War 2 order for an English system. It proved that single truck comfort was achieveable, but a decade later the fine system was no more. (6.6.51)

Above: At Middlewood car No 65, built 1927, passes Roberts No 511 of 1950 design. Older cars continued to be painted with full striping, but Roberts cars had a simplified scheme. (6.6.51)

Left: Almost brand new Sheffield No 511 lays over at Middlewood. The 35 Roberts cars were among the best British single-truckers. The last was delivered in 1952, but the Sheffield system closed in 1960. (6.6.51)

Below: Standard car No 35 of 1927 vintage climbs Abbey Lane to Woodseats. The tryout green paint scheme soon reverted to navy blue and cream that made the cars the smartest in Britain. The neat right-of-way fits well into the modern suburb. (21.9.52)

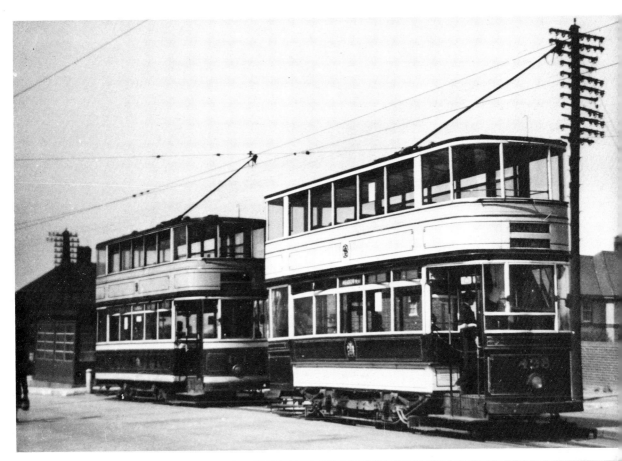

Above: Standard cars Nos 498 (right) and 101 betray family likeness at Lane Top. They date from 1926 and 1930. The top deck bears the transport department cypher, the lower the city crest. (6.6.51)

Right: Roberts car No 511 shows its clean lines at Eccleshall soon after entering service. Set off by navy blue bands, the cream carries City crest and Transport Department monogram. Ads were not carried until near the end, and then not on freshly outshopped cars. (6.6.51)

SOUTHEND

Above: On Eastwood Boulevard, trolleybus No 124 heads for central Southend eight weeks before closure of the sole remaining western circular route. The designation Boulevard is rare in Britain. No 124 was built in 1939 with Strachans body on an AEC chassis and later sold to Doncaster. (12.9.54)

Top right: Sunbeam trolleybus No 146 traverses Eastwood Boulevard on circular route 28B. No 146 had a Park Royal body and came in 1950 from Wolverhampton. (12.9.54)

Right: Light blue and white trolleybus No 127 lays over at the town terminus before leaving for Southchurch. No 127 was built in 1939 with Strachans body on an AEC chassis. Trolleybuses started in 1925 together with trams on the same route. Maximum mileage was reached in 1939, when the Thorpe Bay route closed. (12.10.52)

SOUTHAMPTON

Right: The crew of Southampton's domed roof car 100 rest over at Floating Bridge before leaving for Shirley on the remaining route. Though 50 cars of this 1923 design were built for Bargate services, opentop cars ran until 1948, a year before the system closed. (6.6.49)

Below: A Southampton domed roof car of 1923 design poses at Shirley depot, whose tracks are accessed by a fan laid in a residential street. When the system closed seven months later, many of these cars were sold to Leeds. (6.6.49)